WHERE WE LIVE

Mapping Neighborhoods of Kids Around the Globe

Written by
Margriet Ruurs

Illustrated by
Wenjia Tang

Kids Can Press

This book is dedicated to the children and their families who shared their stories. May you always live in a safe and happy place. — M.R.

To my wonderful parents — W.T.

Acknowledgments

This book would not have been possible without the help of the children featured in these pages. A huge thank you to all of them. In addition, I thank friends and families who made all the research possible: Poleak Chhet (Cambodia); Nico, Aidan and their parents (Canada), Macarena Villarreal (Chile), Rachel Goss (China), Maureen Goodwin and the students of Junior 2 Class at Omoka School (Cook Islands), Reham Basatwy and Josianne Fitzgerald (Egypt); Martha Langille and Tigist Baba (Ethiopia); Graciela Galeano and Jesse Giles (Honduras), Philippa Tattersall and Rajinder Singh (India), Farin Mendis and Fern Cresswell (Netherlands), Basarat Kazim and Anook Kureshi (Pakistan), Stacey Socholotuk and Alexandru Savu (Romania), Yeni Sanchez (Spain and Venezuela), Vera Broekhuysen (United States), and Kelly Geoghegan and Waterberry Zambezi Lodge (Zambia).

Special thanks to Katie Scott for coming on this journey with me.

Published in Canada and the U.S. by Kids Can Press Ltd.
25 Dockside Drive, Toronto, ON M5A 0B5

Kids Can Press is a Corus Entertainment Inc. company

www.kidscanpress.com

The artwork in this book was rendered digitally.
The text is set in Andis.

Edited by Katie Scott
Designed by Andrew Dupuis

Printed and bound in Malaysia in 3/2022 by Times Offset Malaysia

CM 22 0 9 8 7 6 5 4 3 2 1

FSC
www.fsc.org
MIX
Paper from
responsible sources
FSC® C001507

Library and Archives Canada Cataloguing in Publication

Title: Where we live : mapping neighborhoods of kids around the globe /
written by Margriet Ruurs, illustrated by Wenjia Tang.
Names: Ruurs, Margriet, author. | Tang, Wenjia, illustrator.
Identifiers: Canadiana 20210363517 | ISBN 9781525301377 (hardcover)
Subjects: LCSH: Neighborhoods — Maps. | LCSH: Neighborhoods — Juvenile literature. | LCSH: Communities — Maps. | LCSH: Communities — Juvenile literature. | LCSH: Human settlements — Maps. | LCSH: Human settlements — Juvenile literature. | LCSH: Community life — Juvenile literature.
Classification: LCC HM761 .R88 2022 | DDC j307 — dc23

Kids Can Press gratefully acknowledges that the land on which our office is located is the traditional territory of many nations, including the Mississaugas of the Credit, the Anishnabeg, the Chippewa, the Haudenosaunee and the Wendat peoples, and is now home to many diverse First Nations, Inuit and Métis peoples.

We thank the Government of Ontario, through Ontario Creates, the Ontario Arts Council, the Canada Council for the Arts, and the Government of Canada for supporting our publishing activity.

CONTENTS

WELCOME TO THE NEIGHBORHOOD!

The world is filled with so many interesting and unique communities. Some neighborhoods are found in big cities, with traffic, shops and towering skyscrapers. Others are small communities on remote islands that can only be reached by boat. No matter where you live, your neighborhood is filled with the places that are important to you and your family.

In this book, you'll get to explore the maps of real neighborhoods from around the world — and meet the kids who live there. Each story is based on interviews with real kids for whom *community* means something different. But you'll soon discover they have many things in common, such as having families, homes and places to learn and play. You may even find something they have in common with you!

ALL ABOUT MAPS

Imagine being plopped down in an unfamiliar city — without access to a cell phone or its helpful map apps. How would you know where to go? Would you think to look for a paper map to help you navigate?

Maps can tell us a lot about a place. They can show us the roads, landmarks like schools and hospitals, and features of the environment like rivers and mountains. Whether digital or physical, all maps have a few key features, which you'll find throughout the neighborhood maps in this book.

Compass Rose

A compass rose is a symbol that shows the four cardinal directions: north (N), east (E), south (S) and west (W). In between are the intermediate directions: northeast (NE), northwest (NW), southeast (SE) and southwest (SW).

The compass rose is usually found on the edge of the map. It's always oriented in the same way, with north pointing up. That way, you can use the map to get your bearings.

Legend

A legend explains the meaning of the symbols on the map. The symbols show where landmarks and features are located. Here are a few of the symbols you'll find in this book:

- 🏠 home
- 🎓 school
- 🍎 grocery store
- 📖 library
- ～ river
- ⛰️ mountain

Scale Bar

The scale bar tells you how much smaller objects on the map are compared to real life. For example, the scale to the right tells us that the distance between the two notches represents 200 m (656 ft.). This is useful when trying to calculate distances on a map.

200 m

Moana Lives on
Tongareva
COOK ISLANDS

Village population: 225

Moana lives in a small village on Tongareva. This ring-shaped island, called an atoll, is part of the Cook Islands, a Polynesian nation in the South Pacific Ocean.

From an open window of Moana's bright blue home, he can hear the waves softly lapping at the beach. His village has one main road with little traffic. Along this road is a big limestone church — a Christian place of worship — that is over a hundred years old. Moana and his family attend church three times a week, including on Sunday. The school is also on the main road and has about 50 students. Moana's teacher always wears a flower wreath in her hair. After school, Moana swims in the lagoon.

On the wharf, people from the community buy goods from the cargo ships that anchor out at sea. But mostly, they live off the land. Moana is learning to fish, care for animals and harvest and prepare food. The solar farm turns the sun's energy into electricity for most of the village. Coconut trees are used for food, building material, medicine, weaving and clothing — and that's why they're called the "trees of life."

200 m

Aidan and Nico Live on
Salt Spring Island
CANADA

Island population: 11 600

Aidan and Nico are from a small community on Salt Spring Island, on Canada's west coast. They live at their dad's home on a small lavender farm. Aidan collects eggs for breakfast from the farm's chicken coop and picks berries from the garden when they are in season. The boys also live at their mom's home, which is near a lake where the boys like to kayak.

Aidan and Nico's mom drives them to school on weekdays. Their school doesn't have many students, so even though the boys are in different grades, they are in the same class. They are learning to speak French, one of Canada's official languages. When school is over, they take the bus to their grandparents' home.

After school, Nico takes lessons at the swimming pool and Aidan plays at the skateboard park. But their favorite thing to do is walk to the ice cream shop, then along the boardwalk to watch floatplanes land in the harbor. They often see the boat that takes students from nearby islands to school. The school boat is called the *Scholarship*!

200 m

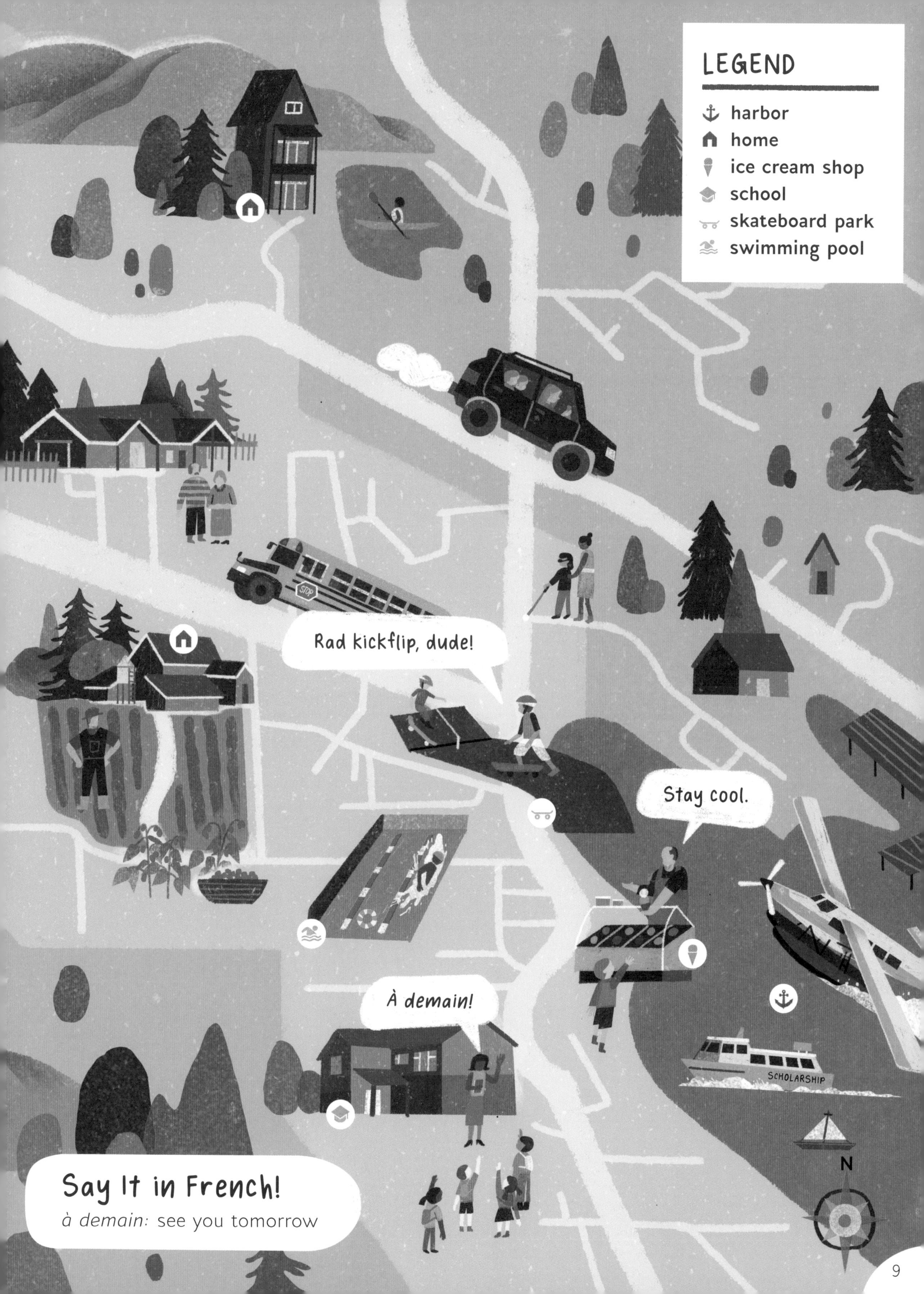

Say It in French!

à demain: see you tomorrow

Jonathan Lives in
Cambridge
UNITED STATES

City population: 121 000

Jonathan lives in the city of Cambridge, in the eastern United States, with his mom, dad and little brother, Benjamin. Their home is a tall house with shutters on the windows and an old oak tree out front.

When the boys have the day off school, they like to visit the library. It has a turret like a castle and a huge children's room filled with books, big stuffed animals and puzzles. But what Jonathan likes best are the hamsters, Blanche and Tallulah, whose cage is at the librarian's desk.

Jonathan's mom sometimes takes the boys to the Korean bakery for sweet potato pastries. They also shop at the grocery store near their home.

The subway station is just a short walk from Jonathan's house. The family takes the subway to visit Boston's Public Garden, with its duckling statues from the children's book *Make Way for Ducklings*.

On Friday nights, the family goes to their synagogue, a Jewish house of prayer. Jonathan's mom is the cantor, and she leads the prayers and songs in Hebrew and English. After the service, they have Shabbat dinner at home with family and friends.

400 m

Alexandra Lives in
Nueva Esperanza
HONDURAS

Village population: 550

Alexandra's small village is called Nueva Esperanza, located in the green hills of Honduras. She shares a home with her parents, grandparents, aunts and her little brother, Daniel.

Alexandra walks to school, and along the way, she sees chickens pecking in the dirt and lush green coffee bushes loaded with red berries. Her school has just over a hundred students. There are four classrooms, a kitchen and a community center. Alexandra wishes her school had a library. But there is a large soccer field nearby where Alexandra plays.

The school day ends at lunchtime, but Alexandra always has a lot of homework. Once she's done, she plays soccer with her friends in the neighborhood. Alexandra's mom sometimes sends her to the grocery store for dinner ingredients: red beans, cheese and eggs to eat with their homemade corn tortillas.

On a hot day, the family cools off in the small river near their house. Or they visit the vegetable garden that Alexandra's grandfather has planted and pick plump tomatoes or pull potatoes from the rich soil.

500 m

LEGEND

- ✳ garden
- 🍎 grocery store
- 🏠 home
- ~ river
- 🎓 school
- ⚽ soccer field

Refrescante!

Amo el fútbol!

Hola!

Say It in Spanish!
amo el fútbol: I love soccer
hola: hello
refrescante: refreshing

N

Fabiana Lives in
Mérida
VENEZUELA

City population: 300 000

Mérida is a busy city nestled in the Andes mountain range. From her home, Fabiana can see the snowcapped peak of Pico Bolívar, Venezuela's highest mountain. Mérida also has the highest cable car in the world, and Fabiana has ridden it all the way to the top of the line!

Fabiana's school is a big, three-story building, and to get there, she either takes the school bus or is driven by her parents. Her favorite parts of the school day are computer class and gym — and also recess, when she gets to play outside with her friends.

Once a week, Fabiana's mom picks her up after school and they walk to the nearby dance studio. Fabiana is learning traditional Venezuelan dances, such as joropo. On the way home, they stop at the ice cream shop.

The whole family shares the same home: Fabiana and her parents live on the second floor, and Fabiana's grandparents live on the first floor. Every night, they all gather for dinner. They often eat arepas (a kind of corn pancake), empanadas (a pastry typically stuffed with meat and vegetables) and sliced plantains.

600 m

LEGEND
- 🤸 dance studio
- 🏠 home
- 🍦 ice cream shop
- 🔺 mountain
- 🎓 school

Adios!

Me encanta el helado de chocolate!

Tengo miedo a las alturas!

PICO BOLÍVAR

Say It in Spanish!
adios: goodbye
me encanta el helado de chocolate: I love chocolate ice cream
tengo miedo a las alturas: I'm afraid of heights

N

Bruno Lives in
Villa Las Estrellas
ANTARCTICA

Town population: 80

At the very bottom of the Earth is Antarctica, a polar region covered in snow and ice. Bruno and his family moved here from Chile, to a town called Villa Las Estrellas.

There are only a few small buildings in town, and one of them is Bruno's home. Sometimes penguins waddle right by his house. After a blizzard, tall snowdrifts block the front door, so the whole family has to climb out the window!

In the winter, it's very cold and dark almost all day. When temperatures drop below −50°C (−58°F), it's too cold to go outside. But when the weather allows it, Bruno walks to school wearing many layers of clothing. His dad drops him off, then goes to his job at the nearby air force base.

Once a month, a large airplane flies in to the airport. It delivers fresh produce for the grocery store (since almost no plants grow in Antarctica!) and mail for the post office. Bruno and his sister, Sofi, often get a parcel from their grandparents. No one lives in Antarctica for long, and Bruno's family will soon move back to Chile to be near their relatives.

200 m

Juan Pablo Lives in
Valencia
SPAIN

City population: 789 700

On Spain's east coast, along the Mediterranean Sea, lies the city of Valencia. Juan Pablo lives here with his parents and little brother, Juan Diego. Their home is in a bright white apartment building — its color keeps the building cool during Spain's hot summers.

Juan Pablo walks to school with his mom and Juan Diego in the morning. They pass the fountain and then cross a main road filled with cars and city buses. After school, Juan Pablo plays in their neighborhood park, where there are parrots in the treetops! Or he visits the local library. He has his own library card and checks out dinosaur books to read with his mom or dad at night.

The grocery store is just a block away from the family's apartment. They shop here for ingredients to make their meals, such as arepas filled with ham and cheese for breakfast.

A hot, sunny day means a trip to the beach on the other side of town. Juan Pablo and his brother will splash in the waves of the sea and collect shells to bring home.

150 m

Leaf Lives in
Amsterdam
THE NETHERLANDS
City population: 873 000

Leaf's home is docked in a canal in Amsterdam, the Netherlands' largest city. She lives on a houseboat with her brother, River, and their parents. To get to the street, Leaf has to walk the gangplank!

On the houseboat's deck, the family grows flowers and vegetables and stores their bicycles. Like many people in Amsterdam, Leaf and her family ride their bicycles almost everywhere. They pedal through the park to get to the museum, where they can see paintings by famous Dutch artists, such as Rembrandt and Vincent van Gogh. Leaf's favorite painting is *The Night Watch*, which Rembrandt painted almost four hundred years ago.

Once a week, Leaf attends ballet class at the dance studio in her neighborhood. Afterward, she walks through the outdoor market where there are food stalls selling *stroopwafels* (a Dutch cookie) and French fries.

At night, when Leaf curls up in her bunk, she is lulled to sleep by the waves lapping gently against the hull of their houseboat.

400 m

Ana Lives in
Bucharest
ROMANIA

City population: 2 161 300

The city of Bucharest, the capital of Romania, is almost six hundred years old. Ana's neighborhood is one of the city's busiest districts. Her home is in a long apartment building that takes up an entire city block! The building has many stories, and Ana rides the elevator to get to her family's apartment.

In the morning, Ana walks to school with her mom and her siblings, Naomi and David. Their school has almost a thousand students — more than can fit in the building at once. So half the students go to school in the morning, and the other half go in the afternoon.

On weekends, Ana and her sister take lessons at the swimming pool at a nearby high school. When the weather is nice, they walk there through the big park in their neighborhood.

On Sunday mornings, Ana and her family go to a Christian church — Ana's parents attend mass, and the kids go to Sunday school. The women at church wear blouses embroidered with flowers, a tradition in Romania.

100 m

Rejan Lives in
Cairo
EGYPT

City population: 10 030 000

The Nile River, the longest river in the world, is just a few blocks from Rejan's home. She lives with her family in an apartment in Cairo, the capital of Egypt. Across the river are the pyramids of Giza. They were built more than four thousand years ago to bury the mummies of Ancient Egyptian rulers, called pharaohs.

Along the Nile is the corniche, a main road lined with palm trees. Rejan likes to watch the feluccas, traditional wooden sailboats, as they slowly float down the mighty river.

Next door to where the family lives is a mosque, a Muslim place of worship. It has a tower called a minaret. Every day before dawn, the muezzin chants his call to prayer, breaking the night's silence. On Fridays, the first day of the weekend in most Muslim countries, Rejan accompanies her mother to the mosque. They use a different entrance from the men and remove their shoes at the door. Rejan covers her hair and prays to Allah on her prayer rug.

NILE RIVER

200 m

Anani Lives in
Addis Ababa
ETHIOPIA
City population: 5 228 000

The streets of Anani's neighborhood in Addis Ababa, Ethiopia's capital, are like a grid. They don't have names, but Anani knows his way around. At one end of the grid is the Orthodox church, where his family attends mass on Sundays. At the opposite end is the mosque. From their home, the family can hear the church bells and also the muezzin's call to prayer five times a day.

Anani's school is at the top of the grid. On the way to school in the morning, Anani and his mom pass the bakery, where they can smell warm *bombolino* (donuts). After dropping off Anani, his mom waits at the bus stop to get to work. Her job is at an international school on the other side of the big city.

In the evenings, family, friends and neighbors gather for a coffee ceremony outside Anani's house. His mother wears a traditional white cotton dress while she roasts and grinds the coffee beans. Anani serves tiny cups to their guests as they talk about important matters in the community.

200 m

Say It in Amharic!

gagarī: baker
salaam: peace (a way to say "hello")

Namisha Lives in
Komanyana
ZAMBIA

Village Population: 200

Komanyana is a small village in southern Zambia. Like most in the village, Namisha lives in a clay home without electricity. People here go to bed when it's dark and wake up with the sun.

The village's school has bright yellow walls and a community library filled with thousands of children's books. Namisha goes to class most days, except if there is a hippo sighting and it's too dangerous for her to walk to school.

Namisha's mom has a job picking tobacco leaves at the plantation, and her dad works at the fish farm. Her grandmother stays home to clean, cook and take care of Namisha's little cousins. Every day, her grandmother walks down to the borehole, where she pumps clean water and catches up with neighbors on all the latest news.

The Zambezi River is an important part of the community, too. It's a place to fish and to wash clothing and dishes. Namisha swims here on hot summer days, when temperatures can reach 40°C (104°F). But she avoids the river during the wet season, when there are crocodiles in the water.

400 m

Say It in Tonga!
kamwamba: hello
muli buti: How are you?
twalumba: thank you
LEGEND
borehole
fish farm
home
library
plantation
river
school
Twalumba!
Kamwamba
Muli buti?
ZAMBEZI RIVER
N

Aimen Lives in
Lahore
PAKISTAN

City population: 11 120 000

Aimen lives in the noisy, bustling city of Lahore, Pakistan's second-largest metropolis. The streets near her home are filled with honking cars and motorbikes, camels and braying donkeys pulling carts. The muezzin's chant from the mosque, calling people to prayer five times a day, mingles with the sounds of the neighborhood.

On school days, Aimen wears her uniform: white pants and a bright blue tunic called a *shalwar kameez*, and a spotless white headscarf. Her school is very close to home, and she walks there with her friends. Along the way, they sometimes hear ambulances, sirens blaring, headed to the nearby hospital.

In Aimen's neighborhood is part of the long canal that runs through the entire city. A barber sets up his chair along the bank to give customers haircuts. Near the canal is a spice shop that sells cinnamon, cumin, cardamom and many other cooking spices. Aimen's mom uses them to make biryani, a popular dish in Pakistan made with rice and meat. There is also a fruit stand where Aimen buys her favorite treat: fresh mangoes and strawberries.

200 m

Say It in Urdu!

khoob parho: study hard
mazedaar: delicious
subha bakhair: good morning
Thoray aur chotae. Mehrbani sae!: Just a bit shorter, please!

Arshita Lives in
Naddi
INDIA

Village population: 1200

Nestled between the snowcapped peaks of the Himalayan mountains, the world's highest mountain range, is Naddi in northern India. Arshita's home is on this small village's main road. She lives here with her parents, little brother, auntie and grandparents. Her family has a pet dog and a cow that provides fresh milk.

On that same road is the grocery store where the family buys rice and vegetables — two staples of Indian cooking. There is also a clothing shop that sells clothes for the cold climate, such as warm socks made from yak wool.

The school is just outside the village. To get there, Arshita walks with her grandmother along a steep, narrow path through the forest. At recess, Arshita and her classmates enjoy the playground. After school, there's always homework to do.

The family regularly visits the Hindu temple in their community. It's located on a peaceful lake surrounded by forest. Arshita will bring a bundle of incense to burn in the temple. She can also buy a garland of orange marigolds to leave as a gift for the Hindu goddess Shashthi, the protector of children.

Namaste.

150 m

32

Say It in Hindi!

jug jug jiyo: may you live a long and healthy life
namaste: hello

Yáo Yáo Lives in
Beijing
CHINA

City population: 21 542 000

Yáo Yáo's home is in a *hutong* in Beijing, China's capital city. *Hutongs* are labyrinths of alleyways built hundreds of years ago, and so are too narrow for cars, which were invented much later. Many homes in *hutongs* do not have bathrooms, so neighbors share the public toilets. Across from his house is a small courtyard where Yáo Yáo plays badminton. On rainy days, he stays inside and plays on his tablet or chats online with his friends.

While his parents are at work, Yáo Yáo spends a lot of time with his grandparents. His grandfather walks him to school and carries his backpack — a common way for elders to show kindness to children. With his grandmother, Yáo Yáo likes to visit the huge park in their community. It was built over a thousand years ago and has a lake, temples and even a palace!

Yáo Yáo and his family regularly visit the Buddhist temple in their neighborhood. At the entrance, everyone respectfully removes their shoes, then steps in left-foot first. Inside, they thank and honor Buddha by burning incense.

500 m

Samnang Lives in
Chong Khneas
CAMBODIA

Village population: 6000

Chong Khneas, in northern Cambodia, is known as a floating village. That's because this community is built on a large freshwater lake. Samnang lives here with her mother, father and three siblings. Their home is built on a pontoon (a flat-bottomed boat) that can rise and fall with the water level. It's anchored to the lake bed to prevent their home from drifting away. Since they're surrounded by so much water, everyone here learns to swim at a young age.

All the buildings in Chong Khneas float: the school, the health clinic — even the basketball court! The floating school has a few classrooms and enough space to run and play. To get to school, Samnang rows a small boat that can fit a few of her friends.

It's no wonder that fishing is an important part of this community. Fishing is how many people feed their families and make a living. Samnang's family also buys food from the village's floating market or from a farmer at the rice paddy on the shore.

200 m

AUTHOR'S NOTE

The stories in this book are based on real children from around the world. Writing this book was so much fun because I got to learn new things about kids from all over the globe.

Before I could start writing, I had to do a lot of research. That involved asking questions and looking for answers. I asked many questions of real children, their families and their teachers, such as:

- ✦ **Where do you live?**
- ✦ **What is your neighborhood like?**
- ✦ **How do you get to school?**
- ✦ **What do you do in your neighborhood before and after school?**

I was able to visit most of these neighborhoods to see for myself what they looked like, including the ones in Egypt, China and Pakistan. For the rest, I spent a lot of time on Google Maps and Google Earth, zooming in to see the cities, villages and surrounding areas. The people I interviewed also provided photographs of the places in their neighborhoods.

When looking for information online, I can't just believe the first source I see. My rule for online research is that I need to find the information from at least three different trustworthy sources, such as museum, university or government websites, before believing it might be correct. The sources that were most valuable in researching this book were the Smithsonian Institution (www.si.edu) and the CIA World Factbook (www.cia.gov/the-world-factbook).

I also asked local experts to verify my research. A huge thank you to everyone who lent their knowledge and expertise to this book!

To Learn More

Mizielińska, Aleksandra, and Daniel Mizieliński. *Maps*. London: Big Picture Press, 2013.

Ritchie, Scot. *Follow That Map! A First Book of Mapping Skills*. Toronto: Kids Can Press, 2009.

Smithsonian Institution. *Children's Illustrated Atlas*. New York: DK Children, 2016.

GLOSSARY

Allah: the name for God in Islam

arepa: a cornmeal flatbread often stuffed with meat or cheese, traditional to South American cuisine

atoll: a ring-shaped island made of coral surrounding a lagoon

biryani: a popular dish in Pakistan made with rice and meat, fish or vegetables

bombolino: a donut traditional to Ethiopian cuisine

borehole: a well

Buddha: the founder of Buddhism, who lived from about 563 to 483 BCE

cable car: a kind of transportation where a cabin suspends from a cable, often used to transport people up and down a mountain

canal: a channel of water, made by humans, often used for boat transportation

cardinal directions: the four main points on a compass — north, south, east and west

church: a Christian place of worship

compass rose: a symbol showing the cardinal and intermediary directions on a map

corniche: a road built into a cliff along the coast

empanada: a pastry with a sweet or savory filling traditional to many countries around the world, including Venezuela

felucca: a traditional Egyptian sailboat made of wood with a tall canvas sail

floatplane: a seaplane that can float on water

hutong: a narrow street commonly found in cities in northern China

incense: a stick that releases a fragrant scent when burned

intermediary directions: the four directions in between the cardinal directions — northeast, southeast, southwest and northwest

joropo: a traditional dance in Venezuela

legend: a key that explains the symbols on a map

minaret: a tall tower of a mosque

mosque: a Muslim place of worship

muezzin: a Muslim official who issues the call to prayer

Orthodox church: a place of worship for Orthodox Christians

pharaoh: an ancient Egyptian ruler

pontoon: a flat-bottomed boat

scale bar: a tool that represents distance on a map

Shabbat: the Jewish day of rest, from sundown on Friday to nightfall on Saturday

shalwar kameez: a traditional outfit comprising trousers (*shalwar*) and a tunic (*kameez*), worn most often by women in parts of South Asia and Central Asia

Shashthi: a Hindu goddess known as the protector of children

solar farm: a power plant where solar panels are used to capture energy from the sun

stroopwafel: two thin waffles joined together with syrup, popular in the Netherlands

synagogue: a Jewish place of worship

temple: a place of worship in Buddhism and Hinduism

INDEX

1 Tongareva,
COOK ISLANDS

2 Salt Spring Island,
CANADA

3 Cambridge,
UNITED STATES

4 Nueva Esperanza,
HONDURAS

5 Mérida,
VENEZUELA

6 Villa Las Estrellas,
ANTARCTICA

7 Valencia,
SPAIN

8 Amsterdam,
THE NETHERLANDS

9 Bucharest,
ROMANIA

10 Cairo,
EGYPT

11 Addis Ababa,
ETHIOPIA

12 Komanyana,
ZAMBIA

13 Lahore,
PAKISTAN

14 Naddi,
INDIA

15 Beijing,
CHINA

16 Chong Khneas,
CAMBODIA